Success into Secondary

supporting transition with Circle Time

**Originally devised by
Cherrie Demain and Lorraine Hurst**

**Developed by Links Education Support Centre,
Primary Team**

SAGE Publications Ltd
1 Oliver's Yard
55 City Road
London EC1Y 1SP

SAGE Publications Inc.
2455 Teller Road
Thousand Oaks, California 91320

SAGE Publications India Pvt Ltd
B1/I 1 Mohan Cooperative Industrial Area
Mathura Road, New Delhi 110 044
India

SAGE Publications Asia-Pacific Pte Ltd
33 Pekin Street #02-01
Far East Square
Singapore 048763

Commissioning Editor: George Robinson
Editorial team: Wendy Ogden, Mel Maines, Sarah Lynch
Illustrator: Philippa Drakeford
Designer: Helen Weller

Rosewarne
Learning Centre

ISBN: 978 1 904315 28 5

Printed on paper from sustainable resources
Printed in Great Britain by Athenaeum Press Ltd.

Acknowledgements

We would like to thank the following for Circle Time ideas and the inspiration for activities that helped us to set up this programme: Carolyn Bromfield, Molly Curry, Shay McConnon and Jenny Mosely.

Thank you to all the primary schools in Harpenden, St Albans, Wheathampstead and Redbourn who have been involved in the Year 6/7 project. Thanks to the children whose work we have used and for their feedback.

A note on the use of gender

Rather than repeat throughout the book the modern but cumbersome 's/he', we have decided to use both genders equally throughout the range of activities. In no way are we suggesting a stereotype for either gender in any activity. We believe that you can adapt if the example you are given does not correspond to the gender of the child in front of you!

How to use the CD-ROM

The CD-ROM contains PDF files, labelled 'Worksheets.pdf' which contain worksheets for each sesson in this resource. You will need Acrobat Reader version 3 or higher to view and print these resources.

The documents are set up to print to A4 but you can enlarge them to A3 by increasing the output percentage at the point of printing using the page set-up settings for your printer.

To photocopy the worksheets directly from this book, set your photocopier to enlarge by 125% and align the edge of the page to be copied against the leading edge of the copier glass (usually indicated by an arrow).

Contents

Introduction

The transition from primary to secondary school is increasingly recognised as the most difficult time in a child's school life, a time when they have to cope with more changes than ever before.

"This is a huge, growing area of concern because when the transfer is handled badly it can be a switch off for the rest of their school career."

(Pam Boyd, Director of Education, Hertfordshire)

This programme was initially set up by the Links Education Support Centre, Primary Team to support vulnerable children in Year 6 whilst they come to terms with and prepare for transfer to secondary school. Many changes have been made as a consequence of feedback from children and their teachers.

Feedback from teachers

"The vulnerable children seem less worried."

"Immense support given to those identified as vulnerable."

"I felt the programme was a success and made the children more confident and less anxious about secondary school."

It was clear from this feedback that class teachers were eager to offer our programme to all of their students, partly as a result of the obvious benefits of Circle Time and partly because all children have concerns and challenges to face when moving on to their secondary schools.

"They move from a small school with one form teacher who knows them and their families to a much larger situation with dozens of different teachers."

(Kate Figgs, *Guardian Education* Tuesday June 11 2002)

We now increasingly provide our local primary schools with a whole-class package, which, in conjunction with the class teacher, we implement and run for six weeks. Sessions begin with Circle Time where all of the topics are introduced and discussed. The programme is intended to be used in the second half of the summer term after SATs and to fit around the Secondary Induction Day.

We send the class teacher a short evaluation, to complete at the end of the programme, and children are invited to comment in writing. Below are some of those comments and a selection of the good bits from evaluation forms.

Feedback from children

"I came in on the first Monday thinking it's not going to help me because I'm not nervous. Actually it did help me and I enjoyed it a lot." Emma

"Helped me with confidence and facing my fears, such as bullying." Daniel

"It's fun and I've learnt about what secondary school will be like." Kyle

"Many of the worries I had are now gone and I can't wait for secondary school." Eleanor

"I hope that the programme will stay for many years from now, it was brilliant." Safina

"I am more confident now, thank you." Caitlin

Feedback from teachers

"All children feel more confident about next year."

"I participated in the programme fully, I felt the Circle Times were the children's favourite activity. I've learned many new ideas and will use them next year."

"Interesting opportunity to raise a range of concerns during Circle Time and consider changes involved in 'moving on'."

"Circle Time activities were most effective."

"Well paced activities and the use of praise made the lesson enjoyable for all the children."

"The children liked discussing issues, loved Memory Mats and feel more confident."

"Great visual materials and worksheets."

"Lots of exciting colours, scissors, pens – they were in seventh heaven!"

The present format for whole-class teaching has been used very successfully for a number of years and, following requests from Year 6 teachers, we decided to publish the programme to enable schools to support their students through this challenging time.

We hope you and your class will enjoy and benefit from using this resource.

THE AIMS OF THE YEAR 6 PROGRAMME ARE:

- ☺ To explain what to expect.
- ☺ To think about the things that you are looking forward to.
- ☺ To help prevent worries.
- ☺ To look back at primary experience.
- ☺ To understand better what it will be like.
- ☺ To feel good about moving on.

MAKE THE PROGRAMME SUCCESSFUL BY:

- ☺ Working cooperatively
- ☺ Good behaviour
- ☺ Enjoying the project

How to Use the Programme

The programme is designed to take place over six sessions, possibly weekly, during the second half of the Summer Term. Each session has a set number of tasks to complete and is easy to follow. You can expect these sessions to take approximately one and a half to two hours. At the end of the programme the children will have:

▸ completed the Memory Mat

▸ completed the book of worksheets

▸ received a certificate of merit on completion of the programme.

The programme is designed to be fun and to enable children to share their experiences and concerns in a safe, friendly environment. During Circle Time, the children who feel too exposed to put forward their concerns will be able to listen to others who feel the same way.

To this aim, the weekly session should be run in a relaxed manner and the children encouraged to interact positively, share ideas and equipment and support each other. This generally means that the classroom becomes noisier than normal as the children talk and work. This is a vital aspect of the programme and is encouraged but needs containment, so during the first Circle Time it is important to set up rules and include a non-verbal 'stop and listen' signal (such as raised hands).

In order to make the final book of worksheets with the front cover and Memory Mat special, the black and white photocopiable resources should be copied onto coloured paper or coloured copies can be printed from the accompanying disk.

Best work, fancy writing, pictures and cartoons are encouraged and of course the use of felt-tips and gel pens are a must!

Memory Mats

The Mat is comprised of a series of stars designed to explore the children's memories of primary school.

We advise the following:

▸ Enlarge the Mat to A3 size (coloured paper).

▸ Begin with 'starting primary school' and work clockwise around the Mat.

▸ Aim to cover three stars per session. The class should share their ideas and experiences.

▸ Ask the class for examples such as, "Who can remember their first day at school?"

▸ Encourage the class to make their Mats as individual as possible and to do their best work. Provide each table with coloured paper that can be cut into shapes and stuck over the appropriate star.

- Ask the children to draw and/or write on separate coloured pieces of paper to record individual memories and experiences of each star heading, for example, 'Best friends'. These are then stuck over the appropriate star.

- Encourage lots of colour and creativity.

- Use the school camera or ask the children to bring in a recent photo to be stuck into the centre of the Mat. Some schools take a class or group photo.

- Lastly, children write the name of their primary school and secondary school in the centre of the Mat around their photograph.

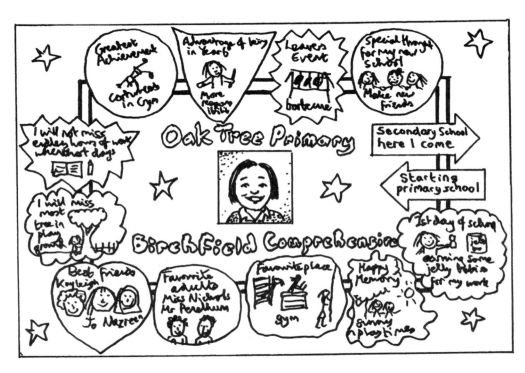

- Once the Memory Mats are finished they look good laminated and make a great keepsake. When in secondary schools we have been approached by children who had completed this programme some years previously, saying that they still have the Mat!

Circle Time

The programme and weekly topics are introduced through Circle Time, which encourages children to talk openly, to respect others' ideas and to have the time to share feelings and opinions in a non-judgmental atmosphere. Through activities and fun games the class have an opportunity to bond with each other and create some more happy memories of Primary School.

In order to encourage this atmosphere some key rules, we suggest five maximum, will need to be suggested and agreed by the class. These can be produced on a piece of paper and displayed in the classroom as a reminder each week.

The class should be seated on chairs in a complete circle so that everyone can see each other and all feel equal.

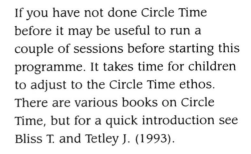

SOME CIRCLE TIME RULES

☺ Listen to each other
☺ Respect everyone
☺ Take turns to speak
☺ Keep comments positive
☺ Opportunity to pass

If you have not done Circle Time before it may be useful to run a couple of sessions before starting this programme. It takes time for children to adjust to the Circle Time ethos. There are various books on Circle Time, but for a quick introduction see Bliss T. and Tetley J. (1993).

The Circle Time will take 30-45 minutes, sometimes longer for the bullying session.

Activity

After Circle Time there are various suggested activities, which always include the Memory Mat except in the final session.

Homework

Homework is designed to reinforce the work covered in each session and to help children prepare for the routine of completing and returning homework to a weekly deadline. The homework record sheet is a useful introduction to the 'planners' used by most secondary schools.

The homework record sheet has space for an individual target to run during the programme. Children should set their own target about something they would like to improve to help them with the transition to secondary (it can be behaviour or work related).

The final book

As the children complete the session worksheets and homework it is easier to keep them in named, individual folders that can be added to. Once they have finished all of the activities, the worksheets and homework can be put together to make a book. We have found that a ring binder works well but treasury tags will do.

A CD is included containing coloured copies of all the worksheets and front and back covers for the book. Black and white photocopiable worksheets can be found at the end of each session.

Have fun!

Whole-class quick reference Circle Time plan

Week	Routine	Activity
1	Warm-up Open forum Round Game End	Clap names Circle Time rules "A happy memory at this school is…" Five pins Pass a smile
2	Warm-up Open forum Round Game End	Clapping word game Bullying web "Bullying is…" Chase the space Chinese drawings
3	Warm-up Open forum Round Game End	Fruit salad Qualities of friendship "I'm a good friend because…" Wink murder Silent tambourine
4	Warm-up Open forum Round Game End	Zoom, zoom, eek Assertiveness role-play with cards "This session I have learned…" Everybody is different Word association with clap routine
5	Warm-up Open forum Round Game End	Silent tambourine Fears, expectations and personal qualities "My best quality is…" Change of identity Sausages
6	Warm-up Open forum Round Game End	Mirror game Induction day "At secondary school I am looking forward to…" Jack in a box Affirmation

The Sessions

Session 1: **Rules**

Resources

▸ **Front Cover** Worksheet

▸ **Memory Mats**

▸ Camera

▸ **Homework Record** Worksheet

▸ Clear plastic folders for holding work

▸ **Back Cover** Worksheet

Circle Time

Introduction to the programme

Take time to talk to the class about the activities that they will be undertaking and what is expected of them throughout the programme. The children need to be aware that, although the programme should be fun, they are expected to contribute, listen to others and respect what they have to say. It is important to set up this concept at the beginning to ensure that all of the pupils feel confident to talk without being mocked for their concerns. It is useful to explain that some worries may sound silly, but that there is always someone with the same worry who might be too embarrassed to speak out.

Warm-up	Clap name. Clap the syllables of your name, i.e. Janet = 2 claps.
Open Forum	Explain appropriate Circle Time rules for the class: for example, we only refer to others in a positive way, we listen to each other, it is our turn to talk in the round when we are holding a Circle Time object, such as a soft toy.
Round	Reflection on Primary experience. "A happy memory at this school is…"
Game	Five pins. The children sit in an inward facing circle. The teacher selects five children as pins. They stand in the middle. At the command "pins down" any or all of the five pins may return to their seats, but they must be replaced by other children so that there are always five pins standing. If there are more than five,

	some children must sit down again. You can change the number of pins in the centre each time, for example, eight or four pins for variety. This game is good for co-operation and collaboration.
End	Pass a Smile. A smile is passed from one person to another around the circle until the whole class is smiling. This encourages good eye contact.

Activity

▸ Complete the front cover. (The black and white version is to be coloured in.)

▸ Start the Memory Mats for the first three stars. Talk through with the children first.

▸ Take photos (or ask the children to bring in a recent photo).

▸ Ask the children to each set themselves a target, which they put on their Homework Record. The target should last for the six sessions, be achievable and if possible have a positive effect on their success in secondary school. For example, take more care with my presentation, put up my hand without calling out.

▸ Set up named homework folders.

▸ Homework: to design the back cover for the book. This should be a self-portrait with a picture of themselves on a bad day and on a good day.

▸ Laminate front and back covers when complete.

Success into Secondary

Name ⬚

Primary School...

⬚

moving to

Secondary School...

⬚

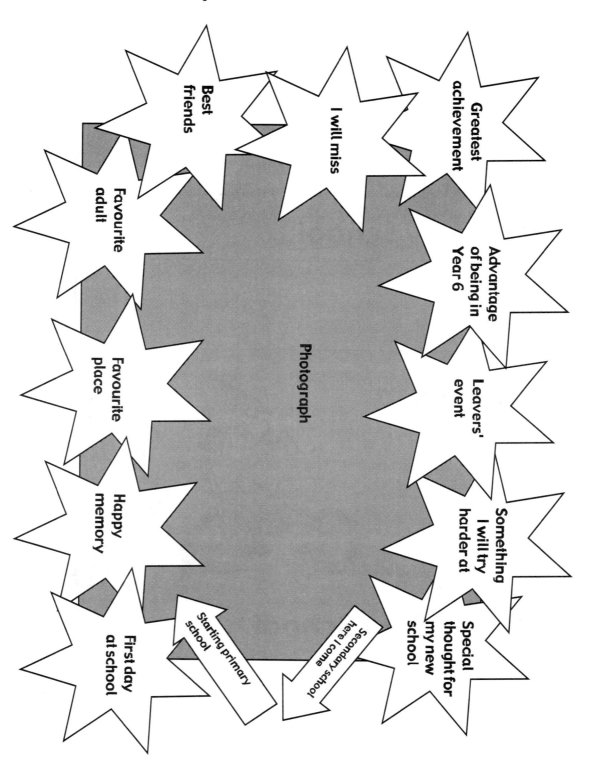

Name

My Personal Target

Homework Record

Week	Homework	Signed	Comments
1			
2			
3			
4			
5			

Me

On a bad day

Me

On a good day

Session 2: **Bullying**

Resources

▸ A3 paper or white boards for bullying webs

▸ **Thoughts about Secondary School** Worksheet

▸ **Experiences of Bullying** Homework sheet

Circle Time

Introduction

Children will need their chairs.

Present a brief introduction to the topic of bullying. Circle Time can take longer this week because children often have lots to say on this topic. Most children are worried about being bullied in secondary school. One of the most common fears is being bog-washed - having their heads put down the toilet. In fact this does not happen! It is important for pupils to have the opportunity to air their anxieties and to allay some of their fears. The bullying web produced in Circle Time can be typed and printed later so that everyone has a copy in his or her folder.

Warm-up	Clapping game using words related to bullying. Each child in turn gives two claps accompanied by a related word, for example, name-calling.
Open forum	Bullying web. Compile a web 'What is bullying?' on whiteboard or a large sheet of paper, then move onto solutions and coping strategies. How do we manage bullies? Who can help?
Round	Complete the sentence, "Bullying is…"
Game	Chase the space. Two children stand in the middle of the circle, leaving two empty seats on opposite sides of the circle. The rest of the class put their hands on their knees and move in a clockwise direction into the vacant seat, thereby creating a continuous flow of movement from one seat to the other. The two in the middle have to try to sit in a vacant seat. The following child is then in the middle.
End	Chinese drawings. A shape is drawn on the back of one child who then has to pass it onto the next person. In turn the shape moves around the circle. (Emphasise that the aim is to concentrate and co-operate as a class). If one child 'feels' the shape differently that is not 'wrong'.

Bullying Web example

Solutions:

▶ Don't hit back – it makes the situation worse and it will get you into trouble.

▶ Don't bottle it up, tell someone – parents, teachers, friends.

▶ Support your friend if they are being bullied.

▶ Assert yourself, say how you feel without being aggressive.

▶ Understand that it is not your problem it is theirs.

▶ If they call you names it is just their way of trying to upset you – everybody is different

▶ Try to hang round with a group of friends.

Activity

▶ Using the Thoughts about Secondary School Worksheet discuss then complete three positives and three worries.

▶ Continue Memory Mat for the next 3 stars.

▶ Collect homework and Homework Record.

▶ Homework: story or cartoon about an experience of bullying. This can be something that they have personal experience of or have heard about. Encourage different genres, for example, poems, cartoons.

Thoughts about Secondary School

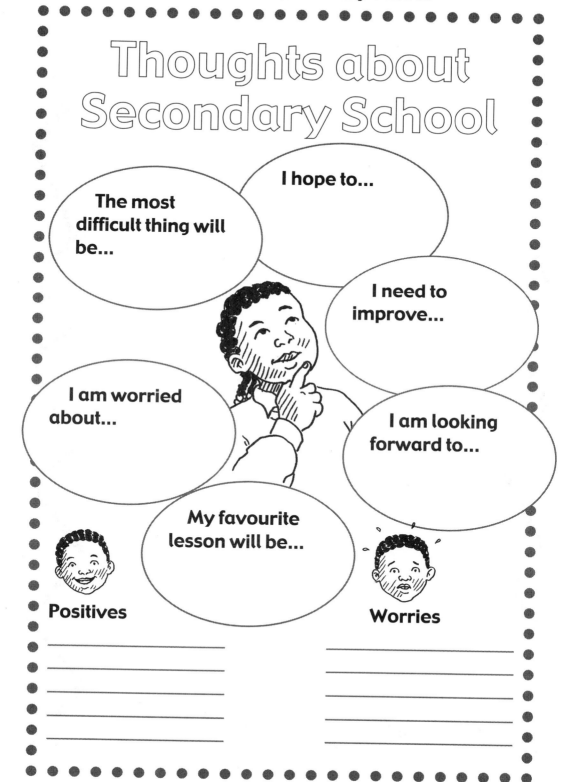

The most difficult thing will be...

I hope to...

I need to improve...

I am worried about...

I am looking forward to...

My favourite lesson will be...

Positives

Worries

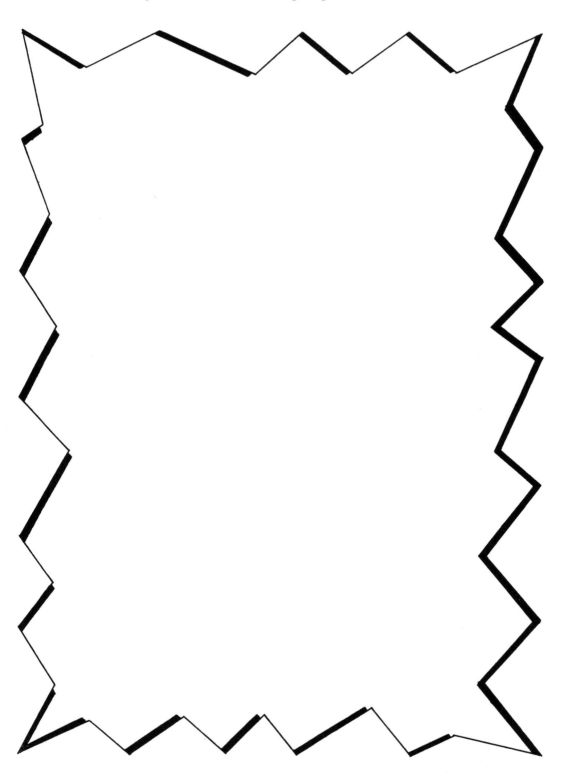

Session 3: **Friendship**

Resources

▸ One card saying '**People see me as a good friend because…**' for each table. These should be laminated and cut for future use.

▸ Set of **Friendship Cards**

▸ **Perfect Friends** Worksheet

▸ **What Makes me a Good Friend** Worksheet

Circle Time

Introduction

Present a brief introduction to the topic of friendship. The Circle Time is shorter than last week because the activities will take longer.

Warm-up	Fruit salad. Each child is given a fruit name, for example, apple, mango, kiwi, orange, banana. Use four or five different fruits. When the name of a fruit is called out those people will exchange seats. When fruit salad is called out everyone changes seats. (This is useful for mixing friendship groups – or undesirable combinations!)
Open forum	Discuss the qualities of friendships, record on a flip-chart or board.
Round	Complete the sentence, "I'm a good friend because I…"
Game	Wink murder. A member of the class is chosen to be the detective and leaves the room while a murderer is chosen from those left. The detective returns to the classroom. The murderer has to discreetly wink at his victims who fall down dead in their chairs. The detective has to discover who the murderer is.
End	Silent tambourine. A tambourine is passed around the circle without making a noise!

Activity

▶ Collect in last week's homework and discuss.

▶ Friendship Cards: divide the class into six groups. One child deals six cards to each child on their table. The instruction is to sort their cards into order of priority as important qualities of friendship. If the child does not like one of their cards then they can discard and pick up another card from the pile in the centre. The group then decides on the six most important qualities to share with the class. Have a class discussion about the choices.

▶ Perfect Friends Worksheet: ask the children to consider the varying qualities they look for in a friend, for example, in the classroom they might be someone who helps and is quiet and on the playground they might be loud and fun.

▶ Continue Memory Mat for the next three stars.

▶ Homework: What Makes Me a Good Friend Worksheet.

People see me as a good friend because...

People see me as a good friend because...

I am a good listener.	I like sharing my things.	I am honest.
I am cheerful.	I try to make people feel important.	I respect other people's opinion.
I have a good sense of humour.	I don't blame other people.	I never criticise other people.
I can keep a secret.	I make others feel welcome.	I am good on the computer.

I'm the fastest swimmer in the school.	I play practical jokes.	I call people names.
I've got blue eyes.	I tell a lot of jokes.	I am short-sighted.
I'm a bully.	I'm thoughtful.	I read a lot.
I'm patient.	I sulk.	I take life seriously.

Session 3: **Friendship cards**

I've got lots of confidence.	I love life.	I smile a lot.
I seldom get angry.	I'm aggressive.	I am polite.
I have good ideas.	I help out with jobs at home.	I always want my own way.
I tell people what they want to hear.	I am a happy outgoing person.	I want people to like me.

Session 3: **Friendship cards**

I tease people.	I am quiet.	I like listening to music.
I am moody.	I've always got money.	I'm very fit.
I don't let new people come into my group.	I'm intelligent.	I argue a lot.
I am friendly with the most popular person in school.	My parents are divorced.	I don't listen to others.

I only like to do what I want to do.	I'm rude.	I'm a chatterbox.
I like messing about in class.	I judge people by what they look like.	I don't smoke.
I use a wheelchair.	I'm selfish.	My dad owns a Ferrari.
I care about others.	I never say anything unkind about others.	I like finding out about other people.

Session 3: **Friendship cards**

I feel I am better than others.	I encourage people to talk.	I have a lot of interests.
I'm captain of a sports team.	I care about my appearance.	I am shy.
I love shopping and looking good.	I feel that I'm OK.	I gossip with my friends.
I gossip about my friends.	I don't have any friends.	I wear Nike trainers.

Perfect Friends

on the playground

Qualities...

out of school

Qualities...

in the classroom

Qualities...

What makes people want to be with me?

Session 4: **Assertiveness and Meeting New People**

Resources

▸ **Assertiveness Role-play Cards**

▸ **Aaron Assertive** Worksheet

▸ **Bad Hair Day** Worksheets 1 and 2

Circle Time

Introduction
Present a brief introduction on the topic of assertiveness and meeting new people.

Warm-up Zoom, zoom, eek. The children sit in an inward facing circle. One child says, "Zoom!" to a child on his or her right, that child turns their head to look at the person on their right and says, "Zoom!" This action is repeated around the circle until someone says, "Eek!" which reverses the direction.

Open forum Assertiveness Role-play Cards. Using the Aaron Assertive Worksheet go through the meaning of what happens when we respond differently to situations, for example, a friend wants to borrow a pen and she lost the last one that you lent. Responding passively, aggressively and then assertively, discuss what is likely to happen. (It has more impact if the class teacher and support assistant act these situations out.) Follow up by the children role-playing a situation from the cards in the different ways (passively, aggressively and assertively). Remind them beforehand that during an aggressive situation they do not touch the other child. The circle could guess which style they are using.

Round Complete the sentence, "This session I have learnt…"

Game Everybody is different. Ask the children to stand if they are in a category that you call out. For example, all children with brown eyes, all children who had toast for breakfast, all children who watch Eastenders.

End Word association with clap routine. Children call out a word, the next child in the circle responds with an associated word in the rhythm of the clap.

Activities

▸ Collect in homework and discuss.

▸ Continue with Memory Mat finishing the last three stars.

▸ Homework: Bad Hair Day Worksheets 1 and 2. This is about conflict resolution. Go through the situations with the children. The homework is to think about who the conflict is with, why it's happening and a solution. The children can illustrate the sheets if they want to.

Session 4: **Assertiveness Role-play cards**

The teacher tells you off for not doing your homework. You haven't done it because your car broke down after swimming.

What do you say?

Someone is always taking your stuff out of your pencil case without asking and doesn't give it back.

What do you do?

Somebody pushes in front of you in the dinner queue.

What do you say?

Someone is trying to take your best friend away from you.

What do you do?

You're in the playground and someone keeps taking the football.

What do you do?

You are a new child at school and being teased by other children.

What do you do?

You are a lonely child waiting to join in with a game.

What do you do?

You accidentally trip another person up and he is cross.

What do you say?

Session 4: **Assertiveness Role-play cards**

The teacher has explained what to do in the next lesson and you don't understand. What do you do?	You're in assembly and your neighbour starts talking to you when it's meant to be silence. What do you do?
You have decided to tell a grown-up that your friend is being bullied. How will you do it?	You have to explain to your teacher that you've left your book at home. How will you do it?
You are lost in school and going to be late for your next lesson. What do you do?	Ask your parent/carer if you can go to a party. The party will be finishing late. What do you say?
Your neighbour in class whispers when the teacher is talking. You answer and get caught again, after a warning note has been put in your homework diary. What do you do?	You have homework to do and your favourite TV programme is on. What do you do?

Aaron Assertive

I express myself honestly and respectfully by:

Standing up for myself

Saying what I want

Respecting the other person

Being confident

> I'd rather not do this now but of course I'll look at it later.

Greg Aggressive

I get my own way at all costs by:

Shouting, blaming, demanding, accusing, humiliating

> I'm not doing this stupid work, you can get lost.

Passive Pat

I hope I get what I want without doing anything by:

Giving in

Apologising

Putting myself down

Hesitating

> Oh OK, I'll do it if I have to.

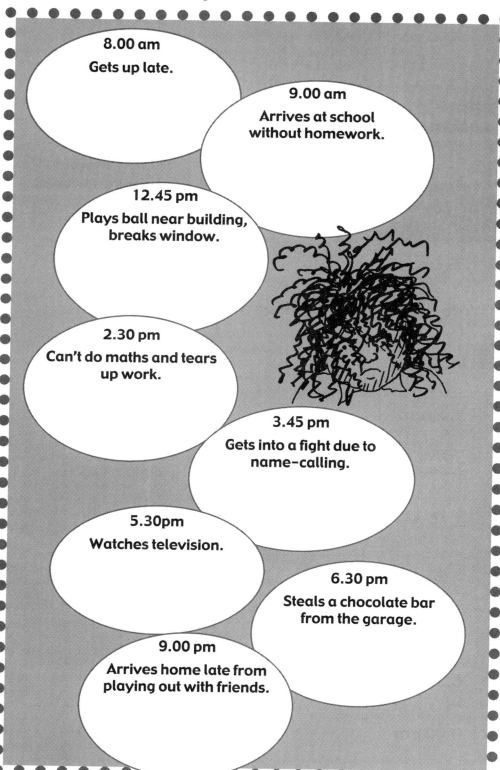

8.00 am
Gets up late.

9.00 am
Arrives at school
without homework.

12.45 pm
Plays ball near building,
breaks window.

2.30 pm
Can't do maths and tears
up work.

3.45 pm
Gets into a fight due to
name-calling.

5.30pm
Watches television.

6.30 pm
Steals a chocolate bar
from the garage.

9.00 pm
Arrives home late from
playing out with friends.

Bad Hair Day

Look at Worksheet 1, someone is having a 'bad hair day'

Think why they might be in conflict in each section.

Think who would they be in conflict with?

Finally, how could the conflict have been avoided?

Write a short sentence for each section

| 8.00 am |
| 9.00 am |
| 12.45 pm |
| 2.30 pm |
| 3.45 pm |
| 5.30 pm |
| 6.30 pm |
| 9.00 pm |

Session 5: **Fears, Expectations and Personal Qualities**

Resources

▶ **Map** of a real secondary school and week's timetable

▶ **Meeting New People** Worksheet

▶ **Induction Day** Worksheet

Circle Time

Introduction

The focus of the session is preparation for the visit to their secondary schools so needs to be planned to take place before the Induction Day. The children might be going to different schools but will all be experiencing the same concerns. If the majority of the children are going to the same secondary school it might be more appropriate to use a map and sample timetable from that school if these are available.

Warm-up	Silent tambourine. A tambourine is passed around the circle without making a noise!
Open forum	Discuss fears and expectations about moving on. What personal qualities will they take with them?
Round	Complete the sentence, "My best quality is…"
Game	Change of identity. The children form pairs. They question each other for several minutes about likes, dislikes, hobbies, interests and so on. They then swap identities. Each child, in turn, introduces herself as the other person and says three things about that child as though she were talking about herself.
End	Sausages. One child is in the middle of the circle. That child must try not to laugh. The children around the circle take it in turns to ask questions, to which the middle child must always answer, "Sausages". If the child in the middle laughs he changes places and the game starts again.

Activity

▸ Collect in homework and discuss.

▸ Map and one day of the timetable: set the children the task in pairs of moving around the school map following the timetable for a day of their choice, using a coloured pen. Don't forget break times and lunch – where do they go? Discuss. Again using the timetable, talk with the class about a typical day, number of lessons, working with different teachers and their personalities and expectations. They are often just identified by initials on the timetable; you may need to explain what initials are.

▸ Meeting New People Worksheet. Go through the worksheet with the children – sometimes it's helpful if there is another adult in the class to act out a behaviour. Divide the class into pairs to role-play the behaviour mentioned at the bottom of the sheet. One talks about a recent event or a topic that interests them, for example, what they did at the weekend, whilst the other acts out the different behaviours. Change roles. Discuss how they felt.

▸ Finish Memory Mat, filling in school names and decorating. The children may need to finish the stars they missed. If possible the A3 Mats should be laminated. Laminating the Mats makes them special and a permanent record for the children to keep.

▸ Homework: Induction Day Worksheet. To be completed after Induction Day.

Timetable

	Mon	Tues	Wed	Thu	Fri
1	Food and N JAL 54	History LWE 15	Geography JLO 18	P.E. NLE Gym	French GMO
2	Food and N JAL 54	Maths ELO 35	English TMR 244	Drama CSO 29	Science EJO 47
3	P.S.E. NBR 31	French GMO 4	P.E. ECL Gym	French GMO 4	Maths ELO 35
4	Maths ELO 35	Science EJO 42	Maths LTA 32	English TMR 24	English TMR 24
5	P.E. ECL Gym	Art RPL 1	Science EJO 41	R.E. PLA 9	Music SDA 30
6	Science EJO 43	English TMR 24	French GMO 4	History LWE 15	Geography JLO 18

MAIN BUILDING FIRST FLOOR

HEAD TEACHER

FINANCE OFFICE

31

30

P1
P2
P5
P4
P3

14 26 25
15
24
23
29
22
16
21
17 18 19 20

27 28

12 11 10

GYM

9
8
7
6

DINING HALL
13

33 32
34 35

38

36

37

39

40

43 42 41

44 46

45 47

48

49
50

51

52 53

57

58

56 55

59 54

CARETAKER

SCHOOL OFFICE

60 61

ASSEMBLY HALL

AH

RECEPTION

5   4 3

1 2

NORTH ENTRANCE   SOUTH ENTRANCE

Meeting New People

It may be up to you to start talking to other people and there are some important things to remember. Practise these now to make it easier on Induction Day – it's a bit like rehearsing a play. Have a chat about the school you come from and perhaps your interests.

Some points to remember

Remember the other person's name.

Smile when you say hello.

Say something positive.

Say something interesting.

Be a good listener.

Make eye contact.

What does eye contact mean?

▷ It means looking into a person's eyes when you talk to them. If you look out of the window or at your feet, what will they think? Will they want to talk to you another time?

▷ Some people find conversation very easy but it is harder for others, especially if they are a bit shy.

Now working in pairs take turns to practise the following:

- looking bored
- looking interested
- smiling at your partner
- beginning the conversation
- looking angry
- making eye contact

How do you feel?

Induction day
making new friends
Talking to new people

Who did
you talk to?

What did you talk
about? School?
Home?

How did the
conversation
start? What
things were
easy to talk
about?

What was the hardest part
of talking to a new person?

Session 6: **Induction Day**

Resources

▸ Small lidded box with mirror placed inside it

▸ **Reflections on Induction Day** Worksheet

▸ **Organised? We can sort it!** Worksheet

▸ **Certificate of Merit**

Circle Time

Introduction

This is the concluding session.

Warm-up	Mirror Game. You will need a box with a mirror placed inside it. Tell the children that you have a box and when they look inside it they will see someone special. Ask if they would like to see the special person. Stress to the children that they must keep very quiet as the teacher opens the box for each child. As the teacher shows each child he says, "When you look in this box you will see someone special." Then, when everyone in the circle has had a turn, ask, "Who is special?" The class responds, "Me." When they answer tell them that they are right. "Yes, you are special."
Open forum	Induction Day. Discuss their impressions.
Round	Complete the sentence, "At secondary school I am looking forward to…"
Game	Jack in a box. First child stands up to say their name, then introduces the two children on either side. When each child is named they stand up and then sit down quickly – hence the 'Jack in a box' effect. This continues around the circle until everyone has had a go.
End	Affirmation. Each child in turn introduces himself and states something that she is good at.

Activity

▶ Reflections on Induction Day Worksheet: complete and discuss.

▶ Organised? We can sort it! Worksheet: Discuss with the whole class, using the whiteboard, which things in their life will need organising in school and at home. For example, homework, sport, carrying books around, use of lockers, fitting in their own life! Look for suggestions and strategies then fill in the worksheet.

▶ Make up the books – these look best spiral bound.

When the maps and books have been bound and laminated the Certificate of Merit should be given to each child. Some schools do this at assembly time in front of the whole school to make it even more special.

Good Luck!

Reflections on Induction Day

Name

My first impression was

_____
_____
_____
_____

The teachers I met were

_____
_____
_____
_____

The lesson I enjoyed most was

_____

because_____

_____
_____

The food was

_____
_____

I am worried about

_____
_____
_____

I am looking forward to

_____
_____
_____
_____

Organised?

We can sort it!

CERTIFICATE
OF
MERIT

Awarded to

On completion of

SUCCESS INTO

SECONDARY

PROGRAMME

signed

Bibliography

Bliss, T. & Tetley, J. (1993) *Circle Time*, Bristol, Lucky Duck Publishing Ltd.

Curry, M. & Bromfield, C. (1994) *Personal and Social Education for Primary Schools through Circle Time*, Tamworth, NASEN.

McConnon, S. (1990) *Your Choice*, Personal Skills Course, London, Macmillan Education Ltd.

Mosely, J. (1996) *Quality Circle Time in the Primary Classroom*, Wisbech, LDA.